Sanjeev Kapoor's
KHAZANA

Desi Mutton

Sanjeev Kapoor's
KHAZANA

Desi Mutton

In association with Alyona Kapoor

Popular Prakashan
www.popularprakashan.com

POPULAR PRAKASHAN PVT. LTD.
301, Mahalaxmi Chambers
22, Bhulabhai Desai Road
Mumbai - 400026

First Published 2007

(4079)
ISBN 10: 81-7991-331-7
ISBN 13: 978-81-7991-331-4

Design: FourPlus Advertising Pvt. Ltd.
Photography: Bharat Birangi

PRINTED IN INDIA
by Tara Art Printers Pvt. Ltd.
New Delhi - 110002

Published by Ramdas Bhatkal
for Popular Prakashan Pvt. Ltd.
301, Mahalaxmi Chambers
22, Bhulabhai Desai Road
Mumbai - 400026

DEDICATION

To the viewers of Khana Khazana and all my readers who inspire me to create new dishes and rediscover culinary treasures.

AUTHOR'S NOTE

Over the years lamb and mutton have attained the status of a delicacy, to be enjoyed only rarely and on special occasions. Once a staple meat of farming communities, it has exchanged celebrity status with chicken, which is now more freely available and much more affordable.

I am often asked about the difference between lamb, mutton and goat meat. Internationally, lamb is referred to as the meat of a sheep which is less than one year old. After that the meat is called mutton. In India, however, what we call mutton is really goat meat!

As a general rule, mutton can be substituted for regular lamb in most recipes, unless otherwise specified. It will have a stronger flavour and require a longer cooking time to make it more tender.

Another question I am often asked is, which cut of meat is best for which dishes. Raan or leg of lamb or mutton is very tender and ideal for roasting as it has enough fat to keep the meat from drying out while cooking. Meat from the shoulder, neck, breast, or shank is perfect for stews and curries. Chops are best for grilling, barbecuing and frying. For kebabs and stir-fries, use boneless leg or neck meat. The secret of cooking lamb or mutton is to marinate it to enhance its flavour and make it tender.

I have compiled in this book my favourite desi mutton and lamb recipes from across

India. There is Inji Curry Kozhambu from Tamil Nadu, Mangshor Jhol from Bengal, Erachi Porichathu from Kerala, Mutton Vindaloo from Goa, Lal Maas from Rajasthan, Kolhapuri Sukka Mutton and the delicately flavoured Aab Gosht from the North. As always, each recipe serves four persons and has been tried and perfected just for you!

Here are some tips on purchasing, preparing and cooking mutton and lamb:

Purchasing:

1 Colour is a good indicator of freshness and the age of the animal. The younger the animal, the lighter the colour. Lamb is a pinkish red colour, while mutton is a slightly darker shade. Do not buy meat which is very dark or purplish in colour.

2 Buy lean meat with firm, creamy-white fat. Avoid cuts with too much fat, or with fat that looks flaky, brittle and yellowish. The more yellow the fat, the older the animal.

3 The meat of lamb is very tender, but the meat coming from older animals has more flavour.

Storage:

1 Store lamb or mutton in a refrigerator or freezer. If storing in a refrigerator, place on a plate to prevent the juices from dripping on to other foods.

2 Lamb or mutton can be stored, tightly wrapped, in a very cold refrigerator for up

to 2 days. Avoid storing cubed or minced meat in a refrigerator – use as soon as possible.

3 Lean meats can be stored for longer in a refrigerator; fatty meats should be cooked sooner as fat tends to get rancid.

4 Cooked lamb or mutton can be stored in a refrigerator for 3 days or in a freezer for a maximum of 3 months.

5 Do not thaw frozen lamb or mutton meat at room temperature. Thaw the meat in a refrigerator, or in cold water.

6 Do not refreeze thawed-out meat as bacteria may develop and lead to food poisoning.

7 Use minced meat as soon as possible, especially after thawing as it is more exposed to bacteria.

Preparation:

1 Wash hands before and after preparing meat. Wash all surfaces and utensils that come in contact with raw meat to prevent cross contamination by harmful bacteria.

2 Remove the papery thin membrane that sometimes covers the meat.

3 Unripe green papaya paste is a natural tenderiser – marinate mutton in the paste for at least one hour before cooking.

4 Marinate lamb, overnight if possible to enhance its flavour and make it tender.

Happy Cooking!

ACKNOWLEDGEMENTS

Afsheen Panjwani
Anand Bhandiwad
Anil Bhandari
Anupa Das
Bharati Anand
Drs. Meena & Ram Prabhoo
Gajendra Mule
Ganesh Pednekar
Harpal Singh Sokhi
Jayadeep Chaubal
Jyotsna & Mayur Dvivedi
Kalpana Deshmukh
Lohana Khaandaan
Mahendra Ghanekar
Manasi Morajkar
Mrs. Lata Lohana & Capt. K. K. Lohana
Namrata & Sanjiv Bahl
Neelima Acharya
Neena Murdeshwar
Pooja & Rajeev Kapoor
Rajeev Matta
Rita D'Souza
Rutika Samtani
Saurabh Mishra
Smeeta Bhatkal
Tripta Bhagattjee
Trupti Kale
Vaishali Parekh
Vinayak Gawande

CONTENTS

MUTTON PUDINA SHORBA

Ingredients

- 350 grams boneless mutton (fat removed), cut into ½-inch cubes
- 2 tablespoons oil
- 1 teaspoon cumin seeds
- 1 medium onion, chopped
- 1 garlic clove, chopped
- ¼ teaspoon red chilli flakes
- ½ teaspoon cinnamon powder
- 1 green cardamom
- 2 medium tomatoes, skinned, seeded and roughly chopped
- ½ cup chickpeas (*kabuli chana*), boiled
- a few saffron threads
- salt to taste
- ½ cup yogurt, whisked

Method

1 Heat the oil in a pressure cooker; add the cumin seeds and sauté till they begin to change colour. Add the onion and sauté till translucent. Add the garlic, chilli flakes and mutton cubes. Continue to sauté for a few seconds.

2 Add the cinnamon powder and cardamom and sauté for two more minutes.

3 Add the tomatoes, chickpeas, saffron, salt and six cups of water and bring to a boil. Pressure-cook for around twenty-five minutes till the pressure is released six times (six whistles).

4 Remove the lid when the pressure has reduced; add the yogurt and cook over low heat for two to three minutes. Serve hot.

CHEF'S TIP

Shorbas or shorvas are Middle Eastern in origin. They are aromatic broths or soups usually made of meat.

PAYA KI YAKHNI

Ingredients

½ kilogram sheep's trotters (*paya*)
1 tablespoon oil
2 inches cinnamon
8 cloves
10 black peppercorns
1 large onion, chopped
6-8 garlic cloves, crushed
salt to taste
1 teaspoon fennel seeds (*saunf*)
2 inches ginger, chopped
½ teaspoon white pepper powder
2 tablespoons lemon juice
1 tablespoon chopped fresh coriander leaves

Method

1 Heat half a tablespoon of oil in a pressure cooker; add the cinnamon, cloves and peppercorns and sauté over medium heat for two minutes till fragrant.

2 Add the onion and sauté for one minute. Add the garlic and trotters and continue to sauté for another minute.

3 Add eight to ten cups of water and salt and pressure-cook for fifteen to twenty minutes over medium heat.

4 Heat the remaining oil in a pan. Add the fennel seeds and ginger and sauté for half a minute, or till they change colour.

5 Add the sautéed spices to the cooked trotters along with the white pepper powder and lemon juice and simmer for ten minutes.

6 Strain the mixture through a soup strainer. Add the trotters back into the soup and cook over a low heat for a few minutes.

7 Ladle the soup into individual bowls, garnish with coriander leaves and serve hot.

CHEF'S TIP

To prepare paya before cooking, roast the trotters over an open flame to singe off the hair and wash well. You can also skin the trotters completely and leave just the bones with the meat clinging to it.

KEEMA BHARI MIRCH

Ingredients

- 8-12 large Bhavnagri green chillies
- 500 grams minced mutton (*keema*)
- ¼ cup oil
- 1 teaspoon caraway seeds (*shahi jeera*)
- 2 medium onions, chopped
- 2 tablespoons ginger-garlic paste
- salt to taste
- ½ teaspoon turmeric powder
- 2 teaspoons red chilli powder
- 2 tablespoons chopped fresh coriander leaves
- 1 medium onion, sliced
- ½ cup yogurt, whisked
- 1 tablespoon lemon juice

Garam Masala

- 4 cloves
- 2 green cardamoms
- 1 inch cinnamon
- ½ teaspoon caraway seeds (*shahi jeera*)

Method

1 Slit the green chillies and remove the stems and seeds. Grind all the ingredients for the *garam masala*.

2 Heat two tablespoons of oil in a pan; add half the *shahi jeera* and half the chopped onions and sauté for one minute. Add half the ginger-garlic paste, stir and add the mince and sauté for five minutes. Add salt to taste, a pinch of turmeric powder and half the chilli powder. Mix well and cook over high heat till completely dry. Set aside to cool.

3 Mix half the coriander leaves into the cooled mince.

4 Stuff the chillies with half the mince and if required, secure with toothpicks.

5 In a separate pan, heat the remaining oil and add the remaining *shahi jeera*. Add the rest of the chopped onions and the sliced onion and fry till golden brown. Add the remaining ginger-garlic paste, turmeric powder and chilli powder, mix well and add the remaining mince.

6 Add the yogurt and cook for two to three minutes. Stir in half a cup of water. Place the stuffed chillies in the *masala*. Sprinkle with some salt, freshly made *garam masala* powder, remaining coriander leaves and lemon juice. Cover and cook over low heat for ten to fifteen minutes. Serve hot.

KEEMA TIKKI KEBAB

Ingredients

400 grams minced mutton (keema)

100 grams. mutton fat

2 medium onions, chopped

3-4 green chillies, chopped

4 sprigs fresh coriander leaves, chopped

1 tablespoon garlic paste

1 tablespoon ginger paste

1 teaspoon. cumin powder

1 teaspoon. garam masala powder

2 teaspoons. Kashmiri chilli powder

salt to taste

½ cup oil

2 teaspoons. chaat masala

2 teaspoons. lemon juice

Method

1 Grind the lamb mince, mutton fat, onion, green chillies and coriander leaves in a mixer/grinder twice till smooth. Mix in the garlic paste, ginger paste, cumin powder, garam masala powder, chilli powder and salt to taste.

2 Divide the mince mixture into sixteen equal portions. Shape into one-inch round, half-inch thick patties and place on a baking tray. Grill for fifteen to twenty minutes, turning over once and brushing with oil every five minutes to get an even brown crust.

3 Serve hot, sprinkled with chaat masala and lemon juice.

NARGISI KOFTA

Ingredients

1 cup minced mutton (*keema*)

6 eggs

4 slices bread

1 teaspoon ginger paste

1 teaspoon garlic paste

3 green chillies, chopped

¾ teaspoon red chilli powder

½ teaspoon coriander powder

¼ teaspoon roasted cumin powder

1 tablespoon chopped fresh coriander leaves

1 tablespoon chopped fresh mint leaves

salt to taste

oil for deep-frying

Method

1 Hard-boil four eggs; cool and peel. Beat the remaining two eggs in a bowl and set aside.

2 Grind the mince, bread, ginger paste, garlic paste and green chillies till smooth.

3 Add the chilli powder, coriander powder, roasted cumin powder, coriander leaves, mint leaves and salt and mix well. Divide the mixture into four equal portions.

4 Cover each egg with a portion of the mince till completely enclosed. Smoothen the surface with moistened hands.

5 Heat the oil in a *kadai*. Dip each mince-covered egg in beaten egg and deep-fry till golden and crisp on the outside.

6 Drain on absorbent paper. Cut each *kofta* in half and serve hot with tomato sauce or chilli tomato sauce.

CHEF'S TIP

This dish gets its name from Nargis or the narcissus flower, known for its dazzling white and yellow beauty. When the meatballs are cut they reveal the white and yellow (yolk) of a hard boiled egg.

KEEMA SAMOSA

Ingredients

Pastry

1 cup refined flour (*maida*)
salt to taste
½ teaspoon carom seeds (*ajwain*)
3 tablespoons *ghee* or oil
oil for deep-frying

Stuffing

250 grams minced mutton (*keema*)
2 tablespoons oil
1 large onion, finely chopped
1 inch ginger, finely chopped
4-5 garlic cloves, finely chopped
3-4 green chillies, finely chopped
salt to taste
1 teaspoon red chilli powder
¼ teaspoon turmeric powder
½ teaspoon *garam masala* powder
3-4 spring onion green stalks, finely chopped

Method

1 Sift together the refined flour and salt. Add the carom seeds and *ghee* and

rub both in lightly with your fingertips. Add enough water and knead into a stiff dough. Cover with a damp cloth and set aside for half an hour.

2 Heat the oil in a pan; add the onions and sauté over medium heat for two to three minutes, or till light pink. Add the ginger, garlic and green chillies and continue to sauté for half a minute.

3 Add the minced mutton and salt and sauté for two minutes. Add the chilli powder and turmeric powder, sprinkle a little water, cover and cook over low heat till the mince is cooked and the mixture is completely dry. Stir in the *garam masala* powder and remove from heat.

4 When completely cold, add the spring onion greens and mix well.

5 To make the *samosas*, divide the dough into eight portions and roll out into oval shapes. Cut into half and shape into a cone. Fill with the mince stuffing and seal the edges. Refrigerate for about half an hour.

6 Heat the oil in a *kadai* and deep-fry *samosas* till golden and crisp. Drain on absorbent paper. Serve hot with mint chutney or tomato ketchup.

Note: *Samosas* can be made using ready-made *samosa* strips (*samosa patti*). Moisten each *patti* slightly and place a portion of stuffing on it and fold into a triangle.

BAIDA ROTI

Ingredients

Roti

1 cup refined flour (*maida*)

salt to taste

1 tablespoon oil

1/8 teaspoon baking powder

1 egg, whisked

Filling

8 eggs

1 tablespoon oil + for frying

1 medium onion, chopped very fine

1 cup minced mutton (*keema*)

2 green chillies, chopped

salt to taste

¼ teaspoon *garam masala* powder

1 tablespoon chopped fresh coriander leaves

Method

1 Add the salt, oil, baking powder and egg to the refined flour and mix well. Add one-fourth cup of water and knead into a soft dough.

2 Divide the dough into four equal portions and shape into balls. Cover with a damp cloth and set aside for a few minutes.

3 For the filling, heat one tablespoon of oil in a pan; add the onion and sauté till light brown. Add the minced mutton, green chillies and salt and cook over medium heat till the mince is cooked and completely dry. Add the *garam masala* powder and coriander leaves and mix well.

4 Roll out each ball of dough into an eight-inch square *roti*.

5 Heat a non-stick *tawa* or frying pan and place the *roti* on it. Place some mince *masala* in the centre and pour two tablespoons of beaten egg over the mince. Fold in the sides to make a square packet.

6 Pour some more beaten egg over the *roti* and drizzle with oil. Carefully turn the stuffed *roti* over and pour a little more of the beaten egg over it so that the egg coats it on all sides.

7 Cook the *baida roti* gently over low heat till golden and crisp on both sides.

8 Serve hot with green chutney.

MUTTON CUTLETS

Ingredients

- 500 grams minced mutton (*keema*)
- 5 slices bread
- salt to taste
- ½ tablespoon ginger paste
- ½ tablespoon garlic paste
- 6-8 green chillies, finely chopped
- 1½ teaspoons red chilli powder
- 1 teaspoon coriander powder
- 1 teaspoon roasted cumin powder
- ¼ teaspoon turmeric powder
- 2 tablespoons chopped fresh mint leaves
- 2 tablespoons chopped fresh coriander leaves
- oil for deep-frying
- 4 eggs
- 1 cup breadcrumbs
- lemon wedges
- onion rings

Method

1 Squeeze the minced mutton between the palms of your hands to remove excess water.

2 Soak the bread in one cup of water for half a minute, squeeze to remove excess water.

3 Place the mutton, bread, salt, ginger and garlic pastes, green chillies, chilli powder, coriander powder, roasted cumin powder, turmeric powder and mint and coriander leaves in a deep bowl. Mix well and set aside to marinate for three to four hours, preferably in a refrigerator.

4 Divide the marinated mince into twelve equal portions; shape each portion into a ball and roll in breadcrumbs.

5 Place each ball on a flat surface and flatten with your fingers into a four-inch round or oval cutlet, dusting with breadcrumbs as required. Place the shaped cutlets in a refrigerator for half an hour.

6 Heat the oil in a deep *kadai*.

7 Beat the eggs lightly with salt and two tablespoons of water. Dip the cutlets in the egg and deep-fry for two or three minutes. Drain on absorbent paper.

8 Serve with lemon wedges and onion rings.

ERACHI PORICHATHU

Ingredients

- 500 grams boneless lamb, cut into 2-inch pieces
- 3 teaspoons fennel seeds (*saunf*)
- 10 garlic cloves
- salt to taste
- ½ teaspoon turmeric powder
- 3 teaspoons red chilli powder
- oil for deep-frying
- 2 eggs, whisked

Method

1 Grind the fennel seeds, garlic and salt to a smooth paste. Marinate the lamb in the paste for half an hour.

2 Place the lamb in a pressure cooker; add the turmeric powder, chilli powder and two cups of water. Cook over medium heat for twenty minutes, or till pressure is released six times (six whistles).

3 Remove the lid and simmer till the gravy has dried up.

4 Heat the oil in a *kadai*. Dip the lamb pieces in the egg and deep-fry till golden brown. Drain and serve hot.

Note: Erachi (mutton) Porichathu (fried) is a delicious example of Kerala's famous spicy dry-fry dishes.

SHAAMI KEBAB

Ingredients

- 600 grams boneless mutton
- ½ cup split Bengal gram (*chana dal*)
- 2 medium onions, chopped
- 2 tablespoons chopped fresh coriander leaves
- 2 tablespoons chopped fresh mint leaves
- 2 teaspoons lemon juice
- 3 tablespoons oil + for shallow-frying
- ½ teaspoon cumin seeds
- 1 teaspoon coriander seeds
- 5-6 black peppercorns
- 3-4 black cardamoms
- 2 one-inch pieces ginger, finely chopped
- 10–12 garlic cloves, finely chopped
- 1 teaspoon red chilli powder
- 1 teaspoon *garam masala* powder
- ½ teaspoon mace (*javitri*) powder
- ½ teaspoon green cardamom powder
- salt to taste
- 2 medium onions, cut into fine rings

Method

1 Soak the *chana dal* for at least three hours.

2 Mix together the onions, coriander leaves, mint leaves and lemon juice to make a stuffing. Divide into sixteen equal portions and set aside.

3 Heat two tablespoons of oil in a pressure cooker; add the cumin seeds, coriander seeds, peppercorns, and black cardamoms and sauté for half a minute over medium heat. Add the ginger, garlic and chilli powder and sauté for a while.

4 Add the mutton and *chana dal*, mix well, add two cups of water and bring to a boil. Cover the cooker and cook under pressure for about twenty-five minutes till pressure is released six times (six whistles). Remove the lid when the pressure has completely reduced. Cook over high heat to dry up the gravy completely, stirring continuously.

5 Remove from heat and set aside to cool. Process or grind the mixture till smooth.

6 Add the *garam masala* powder, mace and green cardamom powders and salt and mix well.

7 Divide the mixture into sixteen equal portions. Flatten each portion in the palm of your hand and place a portion of onion stuffing in the centre. Shape into rounds and flatten slightly.

8 Heat the oil in a frying pan and shallow-fry the *kebabs* till golden. Drain on absorbent paper.

9 Serve hot with onion rings and *pudina* chutney.

CHEF'S TIP

If the mutton mixture is too moist after cooking, add some roasted gram flour (besan) or powdered roasted chana dal to correct the consistency.

KEEMA PATTICE

Ingredients

Potato Covering

- 4-5 large potatoes, boiled and mashed
- 2 tablespoons chopped fresh coriander leaves
- 3 tablespoons breadcrumbs
- 2 tablespoons cornflour
- salt to taste
- oil for shallow-frying

Stuffing

- 250 grams minced mutton (*keema*)
- 2 tablespoons oil
- 1 large onion, finely chopped
- 1 inch ginger, finely chopped
- 4-5 garlic cloves, finely chopped
- 3-4 green chillies, finely chopped
- salt to taste
- 1 teaspoon red chilli powder
- ¼ teaspoon turmeric powder
- ½ teaspoon *garam masala* powder
- 3-4 spring onion green stalks, finely chopped

Method

1 In a large bowl, combine all the ingredients for the covering, except oil. Mix well, divide into eight equal portions and set aside.

2 To make the stuffing, heat the oil in a pan; add the onion and sauté over medium heat for two or three minutes, or till light pink. Add the ginger, garlic and green chillies and continue to sauté for half a minute.

3 Add the minced mutton and salt and sauté for two minutes. Add the chilli powder and turmeric powder. Sprinkle a little water, cover and cook over low heat till the mince is cooked and the mixture is completely dry. Add the *garam masala* powder and remove from heat.

4 When completely cold, add the spring onion greens, mix well and set aside.

5 Flatten each portion of mashed potato on the moistened palm of one hand. Place a spoonful of the filling in the centre and bring the edges together to enclose the stuffing; roll the *pattice* lightly into a smooth ball. Place the *pattice* in a refrigerator to chill for half an hour.

6 Heat the oil in a frying pan and shallow-fry the *pattice* till golden and crisp on both sides. Drain on absorbent paper and serve hot.

MUTTON CHOPS

Ingredients

½ kilogram mutton chops
1 teaspoon turmeric powder
3 tablespoons yogurt
salt to taste
2 tablespoons oil
4 medium onions, sliced
2 teaspoons red chilli powder
1 tablespoon lemon juice
1 teaspoon *garam masala* powder

Masala

1 tablespoon oil
1 medium onion, chopped
1 inch ginger, roughly chopped
12 garlic cloves
5-6 green chillies, halved
¼ cup roughly chopped fresh coriander leaves

Method

1 Clean and wash the mutton chops thoroughly. Wipe dry with a kitchen towel and flatten slightly with the blunt edge of a knife. Add the turmeric powder, yogurt and salt and marinate for one hour, preferably in a refrigerator.

2 For the *masala,* heat one tablespoon of oil in a small pan and sauté all the ingredients for two or three minutes. Grind to a fine paste.

3 Heat two tablespoons of oil in a pressure cooker. Add the onions and sauté till light pink.

4 Add the ground *masala* and saute for two or three minutes. Add the mutton chops and chilli powder and continue to sauté till the *masala* clings to the chops and the oil separates.

5 Stir one cup of water into the pan and add salt to taste. Cover the cooker and cook over medium heat till pressure is released five times (five whistles). Remove from heat and let the pressure reduce.

6 Remove the lid and simmer till almost all the gravy dries up. Sprinkle lemon juice and *garam masala* powder over the chops and serve hot.

SEEKH KEBAB

Ingredients

500 grams minced mutton (*keema*)
50 grams mutton fat
1 medium onion, chopped
6 green chillies, chopped
2 tablespoons chopped fresh coriander leaves
1 tablespoon garlic paste
1 tablespoon ginger paste
1 teaspoon roasted cumin powder
½ teaspoon *garam masala* powder
1 tablespoon Kashmiri chilli powder
salt to taste
oil or butter
2 tablespoons *chaat masala*
2 lemons

Method

1 Preheat the oven to 250°C.

2 Process or grind the mince, mutton fat, onion, green chillies and coriander leaves to a fine paste. Mix in the garlic paste, ginger paste, cumin powder, *garam*

masala powder, chilli powder and salt. Divide the mixture into twelve equal portions.

3 Thread the mixture onto skewers with moistened hands.

4 Cook in a preheated oven at 250°C or in a *tandoor* till almost done. Baste with butter or oil and continue to cook till tender.

5 Sprinkle with a little *chaat masala* and lemon juice and serve hot with mint chutney.

CHEF'S TIP

Do not cook the kebabs till too dry. They should be moist and succulent.

KEEMA PAV

Ingredients

- ½ kilogram minced mutton (*keema*)
- ½ cup shelled green peas, boiled
- 6 tablespoons oil
- 2-3 green chillies, sliced
- 1 teaspoon cumin seeds
- 2 large onions, chopped
- ½ tablespoon ginger paste
- ½ tablespoon garlic paste
- 2 medium tomatoes, chopped
- salt to taste
- 1½ tablespoons red chilli powder
- 1 tablespoon coriander powder
- ¼ teaspoon turmeric powder
- ½ teaspoon *garam masala* powder
- 2 tablespoons chopped fresh coriander leaves
- lemon wedges, to serve
- 2 tablespoons butter
- 8 *pav* or bread rolls

Method

1 Heat the oil in a pan; add the green chillies and sauté for half a minute. Add the cumin seeds and when they begin to change colour, add the onions and sauté till golden brown.

2 Add the ginger and garlic pastes and sauté for one minute. Stir in the tomatoes and salt, cover the pan and cook over low heat for two or three minutes.

3 Add the chilli powder, coriander powder and turmeric powder and continue to cook for another minute.

4 Add the minced mutton and sauté for two minutes; stir in half a cup of water, cover the pan and cook over medium heat for fifteen to twenty minutes, till the mutton is tender, the water has evaporated and the oil separates.

5 Stir in the peas and *garam masala* powder and cook for one minute. Garnish with coriander leaves and serve with lemon wedges and hot buttered *pav*.

6 For the *pav*, heat the butter on a *tawa*. Slice the *pav* horizontally into two and fry in the butter for half a minute, pressing the *pav* down till crisp and light brown.

BHEJA FRY

Ingredients

2 sheep's brains (*bheja*)
3 tablespoons pure *ghee*
1 large onion, chopped
½ inch ginger, chopped
4-5 garlic cloves, chopped
1 medium tomato, chopped
salt to taste
2 green chillies, chopped
2 tablespoons chopped fresh coriander leaves
6-8 black peppercorns, crushed
1 teaspoon lemon juice

Method

1 Clean, wash and blanch the *bheja* in hot water for two or three minutes. Drain. When completely cold, chop roughly into large pieces and set aside.

2 Heat the *ghee* in a thick-bottomed pan; add the onion and sauté for three or four minutes, or till golden brown.

3 Add the ginger and garlic and sauté for one minute. Add the tomato and salt and continue to sauté for two minutes.

4 Add the green chillies, coriander leaves and crushed peppercorns and continue to sauté for half a minute.

5 Add the cooked *bheja* and lemon juice. Stir-fry for two minutes, or till the *ghee* separates.

6 Serve hot with *pav*.

CHEF'S TIP

To prepare the bheja or maghaz, wash the brains thoroughly and boil till soft. Remove all the nerves and membranes.

GINGER MUTTON CHOPS

Ingredients

12 lamb chops

1 cup yogurt

2 medium onions, finely chopped

2 inches ginger, finely chopped

4 garlic cloves, finely chopped

3 medium tomatoes, finely chopped

5 teaspoons green unripe papaya paste

4-5 black peppercorns, crushed

salt to taste

1 teaspoon lemon juice

¼ teaspoon green cardamom powder

¼ teaspoon mace (*javitri*) powder

1 tablespoon lemon juice

1 inch ginger, cut into thin strips, to garnish

Method

1 Whisk the yogurt in a large bowl. Add the onions, ginger, garlic, tomatoes, *papaya* paste, crushed peppercorns, salt and one teaspoon lemon juice and mix well. Rub the marinade into the chops.

2 Arrange the chops in a non-stick pan, pour the marinade over, cover and leave to marinate for two hours, preferably in a refrigerator.

3 Uncover the pan and place over medium heat and bring the mixture to a boil. Lower heat, cover and cook till the chops are tender and coated with the gravy.

4 Sprinkle the cardamom powder and mace powder and mix. Cook for one minute and remove from heat.

5 Stir in the lemon juice, garnish with the ginger strips and serve hot.

AAB GOSHT

Ingredients

- ½ kilogram boneless mutton, cut into 1-inch cubes
- 8 green chillies
- 1 inch ginger
- 5-6 garlic cloves
- ¼ cup oil
- 4 medium onions, chopped
- 3 medium tomatoes, chopped
- ¼ teaspoon turmeric powder
- salt to taste
- ½ teaspoon *garam masala* powder
- ½ teaspoon black pepper powder
- 2 teaspoons coriander powder
- 2 teaspoons roasted cumin powder
- ¼ cup split Bengal gram (*chana dal*), soaked
- 1 cup coconut milk

Method

1 Slit four green chillies and grind the rest to a fine paste with the ginger and garlic.

2 Heat the oil in a pan; add the onions and fry till translucent. Add the tomatoes, ginger- garlic-green chilli paste, turmeric powder, salt and mutton. Stir to mix and cook till the mutton is well browned.

3 Add one-and-a-half cups of water and pressure-cook till the pressure is released six times (six whistles), or till the mutton is tender.

4 Transfer the cooked mutton to a thick-bottomed pan; add the *garam masala* powder, pepper powder, coriander powder, roasted cumin powder and *chana dal*. Continue to cook over medium heat till the *chana dal* is cooked.

5 Add the coconut milk and simmer till the dish is heated through, but does not boil.

6 Garnish with the slit green chillies and serve hot.

DANIWAL KORMA

Ingredients

1 kilogram mutton on the bone, cut into 1½-inch pieces

6 tablespoons *ghee*

½ kilogram yogurt

5 medium onions, chopped

2 teaspoons dried ginger powder (*soonth*)

2 teaspoons fennel powder (*saunf*)

3 teaspoons coriander powder

7-8 black peppercorns

salt to taste

3-4 tablespoons chopped fresh coriander leaves

Method

1 Heat the *ghee* in a thick-bottomed pan; add the yogurt and onions and cook till the mixture turns soft and pulpy.

2 Add the mutton, ginger powder, fennel powder, coriander powder, peppercorns and salt and mix well.

3 Add half the coriander leaves and three cups of water and bring the mixture to a boil.

4 Simmer till the mutton is tender. Garnish with the remaining coriander leaves and serve hot.

ANDHRA MUTTON CURRY

Ingredients

- 500 grams mutton on the bone, cut into 1½-inch pieces
- salt to taste
- ¼ teaspoon turmeric powder
- 1 teaspoon poppy seeds (*khuskhus*)
- ½ teaspoon fennel seeds (*saunf*)
- 4 black peppercorns
- 1 teaspoon coriander seeds
- 1 teaspoon cumin seeds
- 1 inch cinnamon
- 2 cloves
- 2 green cardamoms
- 4 tablespoons oil
- 10 curry leaves
- 3 medium onions, chopped
- 1 teaspoon ginger-garlic paste
- ½ teaspoon red chilli powder
- 2 teaspoons black pepper powder
- 1 large tomato, chopped
- 2 tablespoons chopped fresh coriander leaves

Method

1 Pressure-cook the mutton with two cups of water, salt and turmeric powder till the pressure is released six times (six whistles). Remove the lid when the pressure reduces, drain and reserve the cooking liquid.

2 Dry-roast the poppy seeds, fennel seeds, peppercorns, coriander seeds, cumin seeds, cinnamon, cloves and cardamoms. Cool and grind to a fine powder.

3 Heat the oil in *kadai*. Add the curry leaves and onions and sauté till brown.

4 Add the ginger-garlic paste, chilli powder and half the pepper powder and sauté for one minute.

5 Add the tomato and mutton and cook over high heat till the tomato is soft and pulpy.

6 Add the ground spice powder and simmer for five minutes. Add the reserved cooking liquid and one cup of water and bring the mixture to a boil. Simmer till the mutton is well coated with a thick gravy.

7 Add the remaining pepper powder and stir well.

8 Garnish with the coriander leaves and serve hot.

DUM RAAN

Ingredients

- 1 whole (1 kilogram) leg of goat or lamb (*raan*)
- salt to taste
- 250 grams yogurt
- 1 tablespoon lemon juice
- 6 garlic cloves
- 2 inches ginger
- ¼ teaspoon asafoetida (*hing*)
- 8 black peppercorns
- 3 medium onions
- ½ tablespoon *garam masala* powder
- 4 tablespoons green unripe *papaya* paste
- ½ cup oil
- 1 teaspoon red chilli powder
- 1 teaspoon dried ginger powder (*soonth*)
- 100 grams *khoya/mawa*
- 1 teaspoon sugar

Method

1 Trim the leg of lamb and rub salt, yogurt and lemon juice all over it; leave to marinate for fifteen minutes.

2 Grind together the garlic, ginger, asafoetida, peppercorns and onions to a smooth paste. Add the *garam masala* powder and rub the mixture over the leg of lamb along with the *papaya* paste. Prick the lamb all over with a fork. Leave to marinate for two or three hours, preferably in a refrigerator.

3 Heat the oil in a large heavy-bottomed pan over low heat. Place the *raan*, chilli powder, ginger powder, *khoya* and sugar in the pan with three cups of water. Cover and cook over low heat, turning the *raan* over occasionally so that it cooks evenly on all sides.

4 When the mutton is tender and the gravy is almost dry, take it out of the pan carefully and place on a serving dish. Serve hot.

CHEF'S TIP

Marinate the leg of lamb overnight, so that the meat becomes tender and cooks faster.

MIRCH KORMA

Ingredients

- 800 grams mutton on the bone, cut into 1½-inch pieces
- 15 Kashmiri chillies
- 4 tablespoons oil
- ½ teaspoon cumin seeds
- 3 green cardamoms
- 3 cloves
- 1 cup yogurt
- 2 teaspoons fennel (*saunf*) powder
- ½ teaspoon cinnamon powder
- 1 teaspoon dried ginger powder (*soonth*)
- salt to taste

Method

1 Soak the Kashmiri chillies in one cup of hot water for five minutes. Drain, remove the seeds and grind with one cup of water to a fine paste.

2 Heat the oil in a thick-bottomed pan. Add the cumin seeds, cardamoms and cloves and sauté for one minute. Add the yogurt and sauté till light brown.

3 Add the mutton and sauté for four to five minutes.

4 Add the fennel powder, cinnamon powder, ginger powder and salt and continue to sauté for a few minutes.

5 Pass the chilli paste through a piece of muslin and add to the mutton gradually, stirring continuously.

6 Add one-and-a-half cups of water and bring the mixture to a boil. Lower heat and simmer till the oil separates and the mutton is tender. Serve hot.

CHEF'S TIP

Do not be alarmed about the number of chillies called for in this recipe. Kashmiri chillies are milder than most chillies and are used to give this dish its rich red colour.

INJI CURRY KOZHAMBU

Ingredients

- 800 grams mutton on the bone, cut into ½-inch pieces
- 3 teaspoons ginger paste
- 1 teaspoon red chilli powder
- 1 teaspoon coriander powder
- ½ teaspoon turmeric powder
- salt to taste
- 2 tablespoons oil
- 1 inch cinnamon
- 2 cloves
- 2 green cardamoms
- 2 medium onions, sliced
- 6 green chillies, slit
- 1 teaspoon ginger-garlic paste
- 2 cups coconut milk
- ½ cup chopped fresh coriander leaves

Method

1 Marinate the mutton in a mixture of the ginger paste, chilli powder, coriander powder, turmeric powder and salt for one hour, preferably in the refrigerator.

2 Heat the oil in a pressure cooker; add the cinnamon, cloves and cardamoms and sauté till fragrant.

3 Add the onions and green chillies and sauté till translucent. Add the ginger-garlic paste and sauté over low heat for two minutes.

4 Add the mutton with the marinade and sauté for ten minutes over low heat.

5 Add the coconut milk, cover and pressure-cook till the pressure is released six times (six whistles).

6 Remove the lid when the pressure reduces and simmer, uncovered, for five minutes.

7 Garnish with the coriander leaves and serve hot with *dosa, idiappam, puris* or *chapattis.*

Note: Inji (ginger) Kozhambu (thick gravy or curry) is one of Tamil Nadu cuisine's best-loved mutton dishes.

ROGAN JOSH

Ingredients

- 800 grams lamb or mutton on the bone, cut into 1½-inch pieces
- 4 tablespoons oil
- 1¼ teaspoons asafoetida (*hing*)
- 2 one-inch sticks cinnamon
- 6-8 cloves
- 5-6 black peppercorns
- 4 black cardamoms
- 1 tablespoon Kashmiri chilli powder
- 2 teaspoons fennel powder (*saunf*)
- 1 tablespoon dried ginger powder (*soonth*)
- 1 tablespoon coriander powder
- salt to taste
- 1 cup yogurt, whisked

Method

1 Heat the oil in a thick-bottomed pan. Add the asafoetida, cinnamon, cloves, peppercorns and cardamoms. Sauté for half a minute.

2 Add the lamb and cook over medium heat, stirring continuously, for about twelve to fifteen minutes till the lamb turns a reddish brown.

3 Sprinkle a little water and continue cooking for twelve to fifteen minutes over low heat. Keep stirring continuously, scraping the sediment from the bottom of the pan.

4 Add the chilli powder, fennel powder, ginger powder, coriander powder and salt to taste.

5 Stir in the yogurt and two cups of water. Cook, covered, till the lamb is tender, stirring occasionally.

6 Serve hot with rice or *roti.*

CHEF'S TIP

Traditional Kashmiri Rogan Josh has a thin gravy and a thick layer of oil floating on top. This dish is best enjoyed with piping hot steamed rice. The quality of the mutton plays an important role in this dish. Select mutton with a lot of fat.

MUTTON VINDALOO

Ingredients

1 kilogram boneless mutton, cut into 1-inch cubes

4 tablespoons oil

5 small potatoes, peeled and halved

2 medium onions, chopped

2 cloves

4 black peppercorns

2 green cardamoms

4 green chillies, slit

1 teaspoon sugar

salt to taste

4 tablespoons malt vinegar

Vindaloo Masala

1 inch cinnamon

½ teaspoon cumin seeds

1 teaspoon turmeric powder

10 garlic cloves

1 inch ginger

6 dried red chillies

Method

1 Heat four tablespoons of oil in a pressure cooker and fry the potatoes till light brown. Drain and set aside.

2 Fry the onions in the same oil till lightly browned. Add the mutton, cloves, peppercorns, cardamoms, green chillies, sugar and salt. Mix well and add two cups of water. Cook till the pressure is released six times (six whistles).

3 Meanwhile, grind the cinnamon, cumin seeds, turmeric powder, garlic, ginger and red chillies to a fine paste.

4 Remove the lid of the pressure cooker, and stir in the fried potatoes and ground *masala*. Simmer till the mutton and potatoes are completely cooked.

5 Add the vinegar and simmer for another five minutes.

6 Serve with Goan bread (*pao*) or rice.

SHABDEGH

Ingredients

500 grams mutton on the bone, cut into 1½-inch pieces

2 medium turnips (*shalgam*), cut in quarters

4 tablespoons oil

4-5 cloves

a pinch of asafoetida (*hing*)

1 teaspoon red chilli powder

salt to taste

¼ teaspoon turmeric powder

½ tablespoon fennel powder (*saunf*)

2 teaspoons ginger paste

1 teaspoon *garam masala* powder

½ cup yogurt

1 teaspoon sugar

2-3 tablespoons chopped fresh coriander leaves

Method

1 Heat the oil in a *kadai*; add the cloves and sauté for half a minute.

2 Add the asafoetida, mutton, chilli powder and salt and sauté over low

heat for two or three minutes, or till the mutton turns reddish brown, sprinkling water now and then to prevent scorching.

3 Add the turmeric powder, fennel powder, ginger paste, *garam masala* powder and yogurt; cook, stirring continuously, for one minute.

4 Transfer the mutton to a pressure cooker, add two-and-a-half cups of water and pressure-cook mutton till the pressure is released four or five times (four or five whistles), or till mutton is almost done.

5 Remove the lid, add the turnips, stir well and pressure-cook again till the pressure is released once or twice (one or two whistles).

6 Remove the lid and stir in the sugar and coriander leaves. Cook over low heat for two or three minutes, or till all the water has evaporated. Serve hot.

CHEF'S TIP

This is an express version of a traditional slow-cooked dish. 'Shabdegh' implies cooking which usually commences in the evening and lasts till almost midnight.

GOSHT DO PIAZA

Ingredients

1 kilogram boneless lamb, cut into 1-inch cubes

4 large onions

10 tablespoons oil

1 inch cinnamon

10 green cardamoms

10 cloves

2 teaspoons garlic paste

2 teaspoons ginger paste

1 tablespoon coriander powder

2 teaspoons cumin powder

6 tablespoons yogurt, whisked

½ teaspoon red chilli powder

salt to taste

½ teaspoon *garam masala* powder

Method

1 Cut three onions in half vertically, and then slice them finely into half rings. Chop the remaining onion finely.

2 Heat the oil in a thick bottomed pan; add the finely sliced onions and sauté till golden. Remove with a slotted spoon and drain on absorbent paper.

3 Add the cinnamon, cardamoms and cloves to the oil remaining in the pan and sauté over medium heat till they begin to sizzle. Add the lamb cubes, a few at a time, and sauté till brown. Remove the lamb with a slotted spoon and place in a bowl.

4 Add the chopped onion to the same pan and sauté till golden. Add the garlic and ginger pastes and sauté over medium heat till the oil separates. Add the coriander powder and cumin powder and continue to sauté for half a minute.

5 Add the yogurt, one tablespoon at a time, and sauté till well mixed into the *masala*.

6 Add the lamb cubes, one-and-a-half cups of water, chilli powder and salt. Mix well and bring the mixture to a boil. Cover the pan, lower heat and cook for about forty-five minutes until the lamb is tender.

7 Add the fried onions and *garam masala* powder and mix well. Continue to cook, uncovered, for another two or three minutes, stirring gently. Serve hot.

Note: You can prepare the dish in advance and reheat just before serving.

LAAL MAAS

Ingredients

- 1 kilogram boneless mutton, cut into 1-inch pieces
- ¾ teaspoon roasted cumin seeds
- 2 tablespoons roasted coriander seeds
- 1 cup yogurt
- 15 dried red chillies, seeded and crushed
- ¼ teaspoon turmeric powder
- salt to taste
- ½ cup pure *ghee*
- 1 bay leaf
- 2 black cardamoms
- 4 green cardamoms
- 2 inches cinnamon
- 10 garlic cloves, sliced
- 4 medium onions, sliced
- 2 tablespoons chopped coriander leaves

Method

1 Grind the roasted cumin seeds and coriander seeds to a powder.

2 Mix together the yogurt, cumin-coriander powder, crushed red chillies, turmeric powder and salt. Add the mutton and leave to marinate for thirty minutes, preferably in a refrigerator.

3 Heat the *ghee* in a pan; add the bay leaf, black and green cardamoms, cinnamon and garlic and sauté till light golden. Add the onions and continue to sauté till golden.

4 Add the mutton together with the marinade and sauté for another four or five minutes.

5 Add around three or four cups of water and bring to a boil. Cover tightly and simmer till the mutton is tender, stirring occasionally.

6 Garnish with coriander leaves and serve hot.

DHAABA GOSHT

Ingredients

1 kilogram boneless, lean shoulder of lamb, cubed

1 teaspoon red chilli powder

1 teaspoon turmeric powder

1 teaspoon roasted cumin powder

1 teaspoon coriander powder

salt to taste

5 tablespoons oil

2 bay leaves

4 cloves

4 green cardamoms

3 large onions, chopped

12-15 garlic cloves, chopped

2-3 green chillies, chopped

3 medium tomatoes, chopped

1 teaspoon *garam masala* powder

1 tablespoon lemon juice

4 tablespoons chopped fresh coriander leaves

2 inches ginger, cut into thin strips

Method

1 Mix together the chilli powder, turmeric powder, roasted cumin powder, coriander powder and salt. Marinate the mutton in this mixture for half an hour.

2 Heat the oil in a deep *kadai*; add the bay leaves, cloves and cardamoms and sauté for thirty seconds.

3 Add the onions and cook until golden brown. Add the garlic and green chillies and sauté for one minute.

4 Add the marinated lamb and cook for about ten minutes, stirring continuously.

5 Add the tomatoes and cook, covered, over medium heat, until the lamb is cooked and tender, adding a little water if necessary to prevent scorching.

6 Add the *garam masala* and lemon juice, adjust seasoning and cook for about two minutes.

7 Serve hot, garnished with the coriander leaves and ginger strips.

SAAGWALA GOSHT

Ingredients

- 600 grams mutton on the bone, cut into 1½-inch pieces
- 500 grams spinach (*palak*), stemmed
- salt to taste
- 5 green chillies
- 4 tablespoons oil
- 2 bay leaves
- 4 cloves
- 1 inch cinnamon
- 6 green cardamoms
- 2 black cardamoms
- 1 teaspoon cumin seeds
- 3 medium onions, sliced
- 6-8 garlic cloves, chopped
- 1 tablespoon ginger paste
- 1 tablespoon garlic paste
- 1 teaspoon red chilli powder
- 1 inch ginger, cut into thin strips

Method

1 Blanch the spinach in boiling salted water for one minute. Drain well and grind coarsely together with the green chillies.

2 Heat the oil in a thick-bottomed pan. Add the bay leaves, cloves, cinnamon, green cardamoms, black cardamoms and cumin seeds. When the cumin seeds begin to change colour, add the onions and cook till translucent. Add the garlic and sauté for a few seconds.

3 Add the ginger paste, garlic paste, chilli powder and mutton. Cook over high heat, stirring continuously, for a few minutes. Add three cups of water and cook, covered, until the mutton is almost done.

4 Add the salt and spinach and cook till the mutton is tender and thickly coated with the spinach gravy.

5 Serve hot, garnished with ginger strips.

KOLHAPURI SUKKA MUTTON

Ingredients

- 1 kilogram boneless mutton, cut into 1½-inch pieces
- 100 grams grated dried coconut (*khopra*)
- 5 medium onions
- 3 tablespoons oil + for deep-frying
- salt to taste
- ½ teaspoon turmeric powder
- 1 tablespoon ginger paste
- 1 tablespoon garlic paste
- 4 medium tomatoes, finely chopped
- 2 teaspoons red chilli powder (preferably *Sankeshwari*)
- ½ teaspoon green cardamom powder
- 1 teaspoon *garam masala* powder

Method

1 Dry-roast the *khopra* on a hot *tawa* till light golden brown, stirring continuously so that it does not burn.

2 Slice half the onions and finely chop the rest.

3 Heat the oil in a *kadai* and deep-fry the sliced onions till golden brown. Drain on absorbent paper and set aside to cool. Grind the cooled onions and roasted *khopra*, with a little warm water, to a fine paste.

4 Mix the salt and turmeric powder into the mutton. Pressure-cook with two-and-a-half cups of water till almost cooked.

5 Heat three tablespoons of oil in a thick-bottomed pan; add the chopped onions and cook till golden brown. Stir in the ginger paste and garlic paste and sauté for a while.

6 Add the tomatoes and cook for five minutes. Add the chilli powder and ground paste and cook over high heat till the oil begins to separate.

7 Add the cooked mutton and salt and cook for ten minutes, stirring continuously, till the gravy thickens and the mutton is coated with the *masala*.

8 Sprinkle cardamom powder and *garam masala* powder and serve hot.

SAFED SALAN

Ingredients

- 500 grams mutton on the bone, cut into 2-inch pieces
- 2 green chillies, chopped
- 1 tablespoon poppy seeds (*khus khus*)
- 1 tablespoon grated fresh coconut
- 10-12 almonds, blanched and peeled
- ½ cup *ghee*
- ½ cup yogurt
- salt to taste
- 2 inches ginger, cut into thin strips
- 1 tablespoon *khoya/mawa*
- ½ cup milk
- ½ tablespoon rose water
- a few drops of lemon juice
- ¼ teaspoon green cardamom powder

Method

1 Grind the green chillies and poppy seeds with three tablespoons of water into a smooth paste. Grind the coconut and almonds together into a smooth paste.

2 Heat the *ghee* in a pressure cooker; add the mutton, yogurt, salt, ginger and green chilli-poppy seed paste and cook, stirring continuously, for five minutes.

3 Add two cups of water, cover the cooker and cook under pressure for about twenty-five minutes till the pressure is released six times (six whistles).

4 When the pressure reduces, remove the lid, stir in the coconut-almond paste, *khoya* and milk. Cook over low heat till the gravy thickens and the *ghee* floats on top.

5 Stir in the rose water and lemon juice, and sprinkle cardamom powder over the mutton. Serve hot.

MUTTON XACUTI

Ingredients

- 800 grams mutton on the bone, cut into 1½-inch pieces
- ⅓ cup oil
- 1 cup grated fresh coconut
- 2 one-inch sticks cinnamon
- 6 cloves
- 4 dried red chillies
- ½ teaspoon turmeric powder
- 2 tablespoons poppy seeds (*khuskhus*)
- 1 teaspoon carom seeds (*ajwain*)
- 1 teaspoon cumin seeds
- 10 black peppercorns
- 1 teaspoon fennel seeds (*saunf*)
- 4 star anise (*chakri phool/badiyan*)
- 1½ tablespoons coriander seeds
- 4-6 garlic cloves
- 2 medium onions, finely chopped
- salt to taste
- 1 tablespoon tamarind pulp
- ¼ teaspoon grated nutmeg

Method

1 Heat one tablespoon of oil in a pan; sauté the coconut till light brown.

2 Dry-roast the cinnamon, cloves, whole red chillies, turmeric powder, poppy seeds, carom seeds, cumin seeds, peppercorns, fennel seeds, star anise and coriander seeds till fragrant. Grind to a paste together with the garlic and roasted coconut and three-fourth cup of water.

3 Heat the remaining oil in a thick-bottomed pan and sauté the onions till brown.

4 Add the *masala* paste and cook till the oil separates. Add the mutton and sauté for two to three minutes. Add two cups of water and salt and pressure-cook till the pressure releases six to eight times (six to eight whistles), or till the mutton is tender.

5 Remove the lid of the cooker when the pressure reduces. Stir in the tamarind pulp and grated nutmeg and simmer for two minutes.

6 Serve hot with Goan bread (*pao*), or steamed Goan parboiled rice.

TEEWARN (SINDHI MUTTON CURRY)

Ingredients

- 1 kilogram mutton chops
- 6 tablespoons oil
- 1 teaspoon cumin seeds
- 2-3 cloves
- 2 green cardamoms
- 1 bay leaf
- 2 large onions, chopped
- 1 teaspoon ginger paste
- ½ tablespoon garlic paste
- 3 green chillies, chopped
- 3 medium tomatoes, chopped
- salt to taste
- 1 tablespoon red chilli powder
- ½ tablespoon coriander powder
- ¼ teaspoon turmeric powder
- ¼ cup yogurt
- ½ teaspoon *garam masala* powder

Method

1 Heat the oil in a *kadai*; add the cumin seeds, cloves, cardamoms and bay leaf and sauté for half a minute.

2 When the spices begin to change colour, add the onions and sauté over medium heat till light golden.

3 Add the ginger paste, garlic paste, green chillies, tomatoes and salt and cook over low heat for two or three minutes.

4 Add the chilli powder, coriander powder, turmeric powder and mutton chops. Stir and continue to cook for three or four minutes.

5 Add the yogurt and one cup of water and pressure-cook till the pressure is released six times (six whistles), or till mutton is tender.

6 Remove the lid when the pressure reduces, stir in the *garam masala* powder and simmer for two minutes.

7 Serve hot with steamed rice.

NALLI NIHARI

Ingredients

500	grams mutton marrow bones (*nalli*)
2½	tablespoons *Nihari Masala*
	oil for deep-frying
2	medium onions, sliced
2	tablespoons *ghee*
½	inch ginger, cut into thin strips
2	tablespoons wholewheat flour (*atta*)
	salt to taste
1	tablespoon lemon juice
2	tablespoons chopped fresh coriander leaves

Method

1 Heat the oil in a *kadai* and deep-fry onions till golden. Drain on absorbent paper.

2 Heat the *ghee* in a pressure cooker. Add the *nalli* and *nihari masala* and sauté for two minutes. Add four cups of water and cook under pressure for about half an hour till the pressure is released eight times (eight whistles).

3 Remove the lid when the pressure has reduced and transfer the contents to a *kadai*. Bring the mixture to a boil; add half the fried onions and half the ginger, lower heat and simmer for two minutes.

4 Combine the wholewheat flour with six tablespoons of water and mix into a smooth paste.

5 Add the paste to the *nalli* mixture and continue to simmer, stirring continuously, till the gravy thickens. Stir in the salt and lemon juice.

6 Serve, garnished with the remaining fried onions, ginger and the coriander leaves.

CHEF'S TIP

This is speedy version of a dish that tastes best when it is allowed to simmer over a low heat for several hours for the richness of the marrow bones to seep into and thicken the gravy.

MANGSHOR JHOL

Ingredients

- 500 grams mutton on the bone, cut into 1½-inch pieces
- 1 tablespoon ginger paste
- 1 tablespoon garlic paste
- salt to taste
- 2-3 tablespoons oil
- 2 bay leaves
- 1 teaspoon *paanch phoron* (see below)
- 2 medium onions, ground
- 1½ teaspoons red chilli powder
- 1 teaspoon turmeric powder
- 1 teaspoon coriander powder
- ½ teaspoon roasted cumin powder
- 2 medium tomatoes, puréed
- 2 medium potatoes, peeled and cut into 1-inch cubes
- ½ teaspoon sugar
- 1 tablespoon *ghee*
- 2-3 tablespoons chopped fresh coriander leaves

Method

1 Marinate the mutton in the ginger-garlic paste and salt for about an hour.

2 Heat the oil in a pan; add the bay leaves and *panch phoron* and sauté for one minute.

3 Add the onion paste and fry till translucent.

4 Add the mutton with the marinade, chilli powder, turmeric powder, coriander powder and roasted cumin powder. Cook for a few minutes, stirring continuously, till the oil starts separating from the masala. Mix in the tomato purée and potatoes.

5 Add one cup of water and pressure-cook over medium heat till the pressure is released six times (six whistles).

6 Remove the lid when the pressure reduces. Stir in the sugar, *ghee* and coriander leaves and serve hot.

Note: *Paanch Phoron* is a mixture of equal quantities of cumin seeds, mustard seeds, fenugreek seeds (methi dana), fennel seeds (saunf) and onion seeds (kalonji).

SHAAN E RAAN

Ingredients

- 1 whole (1 kilogram) leg of goat or lamb
- 4-5 tablespoons green unripe papaya paste
- 2 tablespoons garlic paste
- 2 tablespoons ginger paste
- salt to taste
- ½ cup oil
- 6 large onions, chopped
- 4 large tomatoes, chopped
- ½ teaspoon turmeric powder
- 2 tablespoons coriander powder
- 1 tablespoon roasted cumin powder
- 3-4 teaspoons red chilli powder
- ¼ teaspoon green cardamom powder
- ½ tablespoon *garam masala* powder
- 1 cup yogurt, whisked
- 2 tablespoons chopped fresh coriander leaves
- 1 large onion, sliced into rings
- a sprig of fresh mint leaves

Method

1 Clean the leg of lamb and make small gashes all over.

2 Combine the papaya paste, one-and-a-half tablespoons of garlic paste, one-and-a-half tablespoons of ginger paste and salt and rub the mixture all over the lamb. Leave to marinate for two or three hours, preferably in a refrigerator.

3 Preheat the oven to 180°C.

4 Heat the oil in a pan; add the onions and sauté over medium heat till light golden. Add the remaining ginger paste and garlic paste and continue to sauté. Add the tomatoes and sauté for a few minutes.

5 Add the turmeric powder, coriander powder, roasted cumin powder and chilli powder and continue to sauté for a few minutes.

6 Add the cardamom powder and *garam masala* powder and mix well. Stir in the yogurt, coriander leaves and salt.

7 Grease a baking tray and place the marinated leg of lamb in it. Pour the *masala* over the leg of lamb. Cover with aluminium foil and cook in the oven for forty to forty-five minutes. Lower the temperature to 140°C and continue to bake for one hour.

8 Serve hot, garnished with onion rings and mint.

KERALA BIRYANI

Ingredients

- 1½ cups long-grain rice
- 750 grams lamb or mutton on the bone, cut into 1-inch pieces
- 1 cup grated fresh coconut
- ¾ teaspoon roasted coriander powder
- ¼ teaspoon powder roasted red chilli
- ¼ teaspoon fennel powder (*saunf*)
- ¼ teaspoon black pepper powder
- ½ cup + 1 tablespoon *ghee*
- ¼ teaspoon turmeric powder
- 5 large onions, finely sliced
- 10-12 cashew nuts, finely chopped
- 2 tablespoons raisins (*kishmish*)
- 15-20 curry leaves
- 2 one-inch sticks cinnamon
- 5-6 cloves
- 3 green cardamoms
- ¾ tablespoon garlic paste
- 1 teaspoon ginger paste
- 2 green chillies, slit

¼ cup yogurt

salt to taste

2 tablespoons chopped fresh coriander leaves

2 tablespoons chopped fresh mint leaves

Method

1 Grind the coconut with half a cup of water and extract half a cup of thick coconut milk. Set the coconut milk aside and reserve the coconut.

2 Mix together the coriander powder, chilli powder, fennel powder, pepper powder and two tablespoons of water.

3 Cook the rice in four cups of water till three-fourths done. Drain.

4 Heat the *ghee* in a pressure cooker; add the turmeric powder, onions, cashew nuts, raisins and curry leaves and sauté till golden.

5 Add the spice paste, cinnamon, cloves and cardamoms and sauté for one minute. Add the garlic and ginger pastes and continue to sauté for a while.

6 Lower heat, add the green chillies and the reserved ground coconut and sauté for two or three minutes.

7 Add the lamb and mix well. Stir in the yogurt, salt and coconut milk.

8 Add two-and-a-half cups of water and stir. Cover the cooker with the lid and cook under pressure till pressure is released six times (six whistles).

9 Remove the lid when the pressure has reduced and spread the rice over the lamb mixture. Drizzle one tablespoon of *ghee* all over the rice. Put the lid back on without the weight and simmer for ten to fifteen minutes.

10 Serve hot, garnished with the coriander and mint leaves.

Note: This fragrant dish best represents Kerala, the land of spices. Every one of Kerala's array of spices can be found here, tempered with the sweet flavours of its world famous coconuts and cashew nuts.

GOSHT BIRYANI

Ingredients

- 1 kilogram mutton or lamb on the bone, cut into 1½-inch pieces
- 1½ cups Basmati rice, soaked
- a generous pinch of saffron
- ½ cup warm milk
- 2 cups yogurt
- salt to taste
- 1 teaspoon turmeric powder
- 2 tablespoons garlic paste
- 2 tablespoons ginger paste
- 4-5 cloves
- 1 inch cinnamon
- 4-5 green cardamoms
- 1-2 black cardamoms
- 6-8 black peppercorns
- 5 tablespoons oil + for deep-frying
- 5-6 large onions, thinly sliced
- 2 green chillies, chopped
- 2 tablespoons coriander powder
- 1 tablespoon cumin powder
- 1 teaspoon red chilli powder
- 4 large tomatoes, chopped
- 2 teaspoons *garam masala* powder

½ cup chopped fresh coriander leaves

2 one-inch pieces ginger, cut into thin strips

½ cup chopped fresh mint leaves

¼ cup butter

Method

1 Soak the saffron in warm milk and set aside.

2 Marinate the mutton in a mixture of the yogurt, salt, turmeric powder and one tablespoon each of ginger and garlic pastes for about four hours in a refrigerator.

3 Cook the rice in boiling salted water together with the cloves, cinnamon, green cardamoms, black cardamoms and peppercorns till the rice is almost cooked. Strain and keep the rice warm.

4 Heat the oil in a *kadai* and deep-fry half the onions till golden brown. Drain on absorbent paper.

5 Heat five tablespoons of oil in a thick bottomed pan; add the remaining onions and green chillies and sauté till the onions turn a light golden brown.

6 Add the remaining ginger paste and garlic paste and mix well. Add the marinated mutton and cook over high heat for seven to eight minutes. Add the

coriander powder, cumin powder and chilli powder and mix thoroughly.

7 Stir in three cups of water, bring to a boil, lower heat and cook, covered, till the mutton is almost cooked. Add the tomatoes, salt, one teaspoon of *garam masala* powder and the coriander leaves. Cook for fifteen minutes over medium heat, stirring occasionally.

8 If using a pressure cooker, add the tomatoes, salt, *garam masala* powder, two cups of water and coriander leaves after adding the spice powders. Pressure-cook till the mutton is almost cooked (two to three whistles).

9 If the gravy is too thin, cook over high heat to thicken the gravy.

10 Preheat the oven to 200°C.

11 Arrange half the quantity of cooked mutton in an ovenproof dish and spread half the quantity of rice over the mutton. Sprinkle half the remaining *garam masala* powder, half each of the ginger strips, saffron-flavoured milk and mint leaves. Dot with half the butter. Repeat the layers ending with butter.

12 Cover tightly with aluminium foil and cook in the oven for fifteen to twenty minutes.

13 Serve, garnished with fried onions and accompanied by a mixed vegetable *raita*.